P9-CTA-869

Another Kind
of Autumn

ALSO BY LOREN EISELEY

The Immense Journey
1957

Darwin's Century
1958

The Firmament of Time
1960

The Unexpected Universe
1969

The Invisible Pyramid
1970

The Night Country
1971

Notes of an Alchemist
1972

The Man Who Saw Through Time
1973

The Innocent Assassins
1973

All the Strange Hours
1975

Another Kind of Autumn

LOREN EISELEY

WOODCUTS BY WALTER FERRO

CHARLES SCRIBNER'S SONS / NEW YORK

PS
3555
I78
A8
1977

11/1978
Am. Lit.

Text Copyright © 1977 the Estate of Loren Eiseley, copyright © 1976 Loren Eiseley.
Woodcut illustrations copyright © 1977 Walter Ferro.

Library of Congress Cataloging in Publication Data
Eiseley, Loren C —
    Another kind of autumn.
    I. Title.
PS3555.I78A8   811'.5'4   77-8130
ISBN 0-684-15138-3

THIS BOOK PUBLISHED SIMULTANEOUSLY IN
THE UNITED STATES OF AMERICA AND IN CANADA –
COPYRIGHT UNDER THE BERNE CONVENTION

ALL RIGHTS RESERVED. NO PART OF THIS BOOK
MAY BE REPRODUCED IN ANY FORM WITHOUT
THE PERMISSION OF CHARLES SCRIBNER'S SONS.

3 5 7 9 11 13 15 17 19 V/C 20 18 16 14 12 10 8 6 4 2

PRINTED IN THE UNITED STATES OF AMERICA

Four poems in this collection appeared in the June 1977 issue of *Harper's* Magazine; one in the November 1976 issue, one in the March 1977 issue, and one in the May 1977 issue of *Audubon* Magazine. "Safe in the Toy Box" and "Knossus" appeared in the September 1976 issue of *Poetry;* "Two Hours from Now" in the April 1977 issue of *Poetry.*

Dedicated to the memory of a very brave woman
CAROLINE HUTTON ELSEA, 1873–1942

and to her equally brave daughters
HELEN TREAT
ELOISE ELSEA
CAROLINE WERKLEY

CONTENTS

11

Another Kind of Autumn

ANOTHER KIND OF AUTUMN

This petrified branch with the harsh look whose mineralized
                                    splinters are needle-sharp
was living a hundred million years ago,
bent to invisible wind, put out leaves on the mountain.
                                    Today
the mountain is gone and this fragment
lies on my desk imperishable and waits for me in turn
                                    to be gone.
Living once it has taken to minerals for survival.
                                    This hand that writes
stiffens, but has no such powers, no crystalline absorption
to hold a pen through eons while slow thought gutters
from lichen-green boulders and fallen pinnacles.
Ink will congeal and perish, this pen rust into its elements,
the thought here, the realization of time, perish
with the dissolving brain. It appears the universe
likes the seams of the coal, the lost leaf imprinted in shale,
the insect in amber, but thought it gives to the wind
like the season's leaf fall. Where is the wind that shaped
                                    this branch?
It perhaps still moves in the air, but the branch has fallen.
Its unfamiliar leaves are now part of my body
and I let the pen drop with my hand, thinking
this is another kind of autumn to be expected.
Leaves and thought are scarcely returnable. The wind
                                    loses them
or one remains in the shale like an unread hieroglyph
                                    once meaningful in clay.

WE ARE THE SCRIVENERS

I have not seen her in forty years.
She is old now or lies in one of those midwestern
                                    farm cemeteries where
no one remembers for long, because everyone
leaves for the cities. She was young, with freckles
and a wide generous mouth, a good girl to have
loved for a lifetime but the world
always chooses otherwise, or we ourselves
in blindness. I would not remember so clearly save that here
by a prairie slough sprinkled with the leaves of autumn
the drying mud on the shore shows the imprint
of southbound birds. I am too old to travel,
but I suddenly realize how a man in Sumer
                                    half the world and millennia away
saw the same imprint and thought
          there is a way of saying upon clay, fire-hardened,
          there is a way of saying
          "loneliness"
          a way of saying
          "where are you?" across the centuries
          a way of saying
          "forgive me"
          a way of saying
     "We were young. I remember, and this, this clay
          imprinted with the feet of birds
          will reach you somewhere
          somehow
               if it takes eternity to answer."
There were men like this in Sumer, or who wept among the
                              autumn papyrus leaves in Egypt.
                              We are the scriveners who with pain
                                    outlasted our bodies.

16

THE SHORE HAUNTERS

Here in this dry, rocky, fired-out place
one can still see the subsiding shorelines of a giant lake;
                                        one can still see
where the blue mountain glaciers fed it,
                        where mammoth grazed,
                            and now all
is stone and gravel, a Martian landscape
with a few bits of flaked obsidian
high on the bitter shores.

The world changes, that is the lesson, but no one
lives long enough to remember, either man
or beast, and the archaeologist
is an anomaly here. The bones of the elephant,
the sandals in the cave by the high lake shore,
speak to no one in particular.
                        Later, by this great dam
                            in the Poconos
I see the motorboats and think
we will always be here, that the pinewoods should shrink
is unthinkable, but so was this unthinkable
to the shore haunters—beasts or men—nevertheless
it happened, the vanishing ice and the fire
                            like the heart's final
contracting country, blackened cinders, dry beaches,
the unimaginable place.

SAFE IN THE TOY BOX
FOR M. W. B.

Here in the box made to receive them
the little toys have lasted these four thousand years,
the brown-skinned miller does his work,
men beat the grain with flails,
the overseer tallies sacks beside the door.
These toys are not the toys of children;
they come from antechambers in the pyramid,
rock cut, where in perpetual dark
a pharaoh slumbers, knowing all is well.

Safe are his lands, safe in the toy box forever—
the waving palm, the limitless estates,
the baker bakes, in boats the rowers row
by powers of puppetry, by all the strength invoked in
    images
through incantations and the magic arts.
The king sleeps well while dynasties dissolve;
stars in the desert night
shift constellations and tomb vandals rob
the great dead even of these miniatures,
the toys prepared for one supreme event:
to hold time as it was—
the dear lost land. Oh do not weep, dead king,
through blinding cerecloths for the toys long taken.
Strong was your faith, your oxen are led home,
the rowers row to steer you to that place beyond the
    grave.
Here in a far land beneath museum lights
they row against four thousand years to bring you
back to the time that was.
So deep the magic laid upon me by your need
I press upon the glass and seek to guide
the helmsman at the stern. I am held in the sorcerer's field
of an old king in cerecloth who bends time to his will.

He strives to focus me once more under the burning glass
    of Egypt.
Light curves, they say, and everything comes back.
The fixed face of the helmsman is my own.
Master, I am commanded at the oar.
I have already entered your small box of toys.

WIND CHILD

They have just found where Monarch butterflies go
                                    in autumn
those red-gold drifters edged in black
that blow like leaves but never
                        quite coming to rest,
always fluttering
                a little out of reach,
                            disappearing
over the next house, or just making it
                        above the hedge
flickering evasively through the last sunlight,
                        the attrition tremendous,
                        thousands die,
blown to sea, lost to children, lost to enemies but
                        beating, beating on,
speed fourteen miles an hour on a three-thousand-mile
                                    course to Mexico.
                Where is the compass?
                We don't know.
                How did the habit start?
                We don't know.
                Why do the insects gather
                    in great clumps on trees
                    in the Sierra Madre?
                We don't know.
They are individualists. They fly alone. Who wouldn't
                            in autumn
like to rock and waver southward like an everblowing leaf
            over and through forests and hedges,
                float in the glades
                sip the last nectar?
What a way to go, you make it, or you don't, or the winds
                snatch you away.

Fly Monarchs and then, if your wings are not too old and frayed,
start the long road back in the spring. Nature is
                              prodigal in numbers
prodigal of her milkweed children (did they learn to travel
                              from milkweed down?).
But I was overlooked, am really not human,
          would be first a tiger-striped caterpillar
          and then a Monarch, elusive, flickering, solitary
blowing on storms and beating always beating
          to go somewhere else, to another flower.
     Over the fence then. Out of humanity.
          I am a wind child.

THE MAYA

They worshipped time and zeros
                           saw constellations crawling
endlessly above the rain forest,
           marked a leaf's descent,
              a flower closing
                    but knew
time was the god
      added another zero and pressed back
beyond their own beginnings
              erected the wrought stone
to mark a million years before they came
                 a million after,
                    between they suffered
                 joy, the light on a girl's hair
                    between
                 they built a city or abandoned it
               gravely erecting the markers
               nothing personal to commemorate the living,
               nothing to reveal the secret of the dead man
                      masked in jade in the pyramid's heart
              or how long he had slumbered.
                    Add another zero and the cities are gone
                 the people sunk in ignorance,
                  add another
and the sun is out
        the sky darkening.
                   It is all
a secret of the zeros unfolding.
        Behind, nothing,
        before, nothing.
Worship it, the zero, and at intervals
             erect the road markers
             the great stelae

with the graven numbers. What other people
have had the strength for this
                         and quietly
let their hands fall
                  obliterating the secret of the markers
                  erasing the constellations
                         before their disappearance—
a blackboard exercise a god might have envied.
            They performed it
            and vanished.

ASK THAT YOU SLEEP

Ask that you sleep forever, IK, the lord of winds
blow leaves, blow leaves across your thoughts until
tornadoes could not hold them. Why did you think at all,
think, as a child, of toys, think in your manhood, yes,
                                    of gods and girls
all one now in the battering of the leaves
where time and wind and void the Maya count as one
and the grim year-bearers come—old things now lost,
fragments of ancient cults, fragments of numbers reaching
past Christian sanctity. Ask of the year-bearers simple zeros.
Ask of the year-bearers peace on tottering stelae.
Ask the obliteration of all dates that lead
in a great circle to a maze of nowhere.
Ask the confounding of tomb-robbing vandals and their prying
                                    lanterns.
See how they all wink out and IK
brings you to where no candle can be lit, not anymore,
                                    nor day but be
passage of leaves, of leaves, of leaves across infinity.

KNOSSUS

"The Kefti come no more.
They bear us no more the oils
and the cedars for coffins.
Their sails are lost." This was their epitaph
along with the recorded black sky and the ashfall.
Then Egypt forgot the gracious isle of the olives
and the palaces of the seven kings
where athletes somersaulted
over the spread horns of bulls.

They died in one night, the pillars of the palace buckling,
great stones cast down, the galleys
beached on the shore, ruin and ashes
assailing men from the sky.
Thera, the burst throat of the world, coughing fire and
    brimstone
there to the north, its voice like the bellowing of a
    loosed god
long propitiated to no purpose.
We have known it in our own lives—
the fear of the moving atoms, but these people
endured the actual megaton explosion, and their
    remnants
faded from history, while the timeless, practical
    Egyptians
regretted a small loss of trade.

Civilizations die as men die, by accident then.
I have seen on an old maple stump
a sapling attempt to grow.
The Kefti come no more,
but here the excavated amphorae
stand by the palace walls waiting
and the beautiful art
is known in the books of the world.

Something lingers in the air as though it would speak.
The waters are bright blue.
I, whose people were horned barbarians,
admire what was done here. I do not think,
in the rain of the fire to come, we will leave anything
    so precious.
Who will bother to scratch after us upon stone the
    regretful words,
"They come no more."

THE FERRY
FOR CECIL BELL, 1906–1970

The old ones
inhabitants of Nilus
starers at the river reeds,
who wrote the Coffin Texts
and made eternity in the heart of a pyramid
these
they lived long enough
to know the adornments of great kings were stolen
that bequests did not ensure to a later time
pity to feed the god.
In the silent chambers
the sacred dead were desecrated.
Their children, their grandchildren,
descendants to the remotest generation
cared only that they, they, the living
might be fed in the halls of Osiris
and the dead be forgot.
So did these ancient Egyptians
like all men everywhere
elbow for place.

They lived long in that kingdom,
learned hardness of heart by observation.
Across three thousand years
wrapped still in the twilight
between this world and the eternal dream
they forbore the offerings,
saw that all failed save the immortal pictures
inscribed in the tomb,
not to be excised from the walls.
In the end, if successors faltered
if the treasures and the priesthood vanished
and the far aftertime
no longer believed—

well then
the king might repossess his land
satisfy his thirst and his hunger
from pictures. The walls
would magically feed him.

The pictured date palm
the grain that came eternally
from the Nile flood,
his women under the trees at evening
gracefully walking
would be there
and the faithful servitor.
No man could take these
from the walls.
Let the dark ages, storm and violence
murmur and pass overhead
while one lived with Osiris
the everlasting.

Now I, a poor scribe,
importunate, mortal
in a young kingdom whose rulers
build libraries, memorials of paper
recounting their deeds,
I have no taste for this.
The paper perishes or the deeds once bright
dwindle to insignificance
as the centuries pass.
I would I were back in Nilus
I would build
one small rock-cut tomb
and have immured in it
not food, nor companions, nor date palms
but one picture from my walls.

29

It is like this, may the picture last,
a jetty silent in the morning sun.
The gulls have ceased mewing,
their eyes are wrapped in a feathery silence.
The water washes green along the pilings,
but outside
leaving forever, my heart tells me,
is a ferry boat with people laughing.
There is music,
they are concerned with themselves,
they do not see me.

It is my century departing.
The laughter is no longer shared;
the music is strange to my ears.
I shall lie in the rock-cut tomb
seeing only the salt, bitter water
and no date palms for nourishment.
I will drowse undisturbed with the gulls,
seeing the boat dwindle beyond the horizon
and grow faint as air.
The ferry will not return.
This picture only
shall be incised in my tomb.
After five thousand years,
a surfeit of goods is hardly appropriate.
One should fix one's eyes elsewhere.
Eternity has its own fashions.
It is best not to anticipate.

THE ABORIGINALS

They lived another way of life here:
Time was different.
Time dreamed here, time dreamed itself
withdrawn from time, a dream time where men and animals
walked softly and stayed in the same place,
the perpetual autumn of no change. There were no bows,
nothing had been invented, no fired pottery, the people
slept in the stone age like hibernating animals.

                 Beyond them
Egypt built pyramids;
they slumbered.
Rome fell;
they slumbered.
The Maya calculated with zeros and raised stones
                            to mark the centuries.
The aboriginals slept with their dogs;
they remained in the dream time, the perfect balance;
their brows were heavy, a lost people,
time had lost them.
They made out with a few flints like the Old Ones.

Why could not life have gone on forever in the autumn country?
Why did those others who came with sails
                       through the Barrier Reef
have to awaken time and destroy the world,
         the unseen necessary balance?
         Why? why?

MEN HAVE THEIR TIMES

Why did the ruins fall so happily,
the plaster scale, the carven jaguar
recede beneath a covering of green leaves,
why are the date-stones toppled, pavements plunged
into the bitter lake, not to emerge?
Why did great pyramids revert to hills
their steps all covered by the creeping vine?
Why do the thousands go, the toilers there
fade into centuries without a name?
Great bowls lie cracked, but no man with a sword
would hack and hack with such persistence here.
The jungle did it and in other lands
                    the sands have buried
what they choose to keep. Men have their times
in little centuries for arts and fabulous monsters.

                    Then there comes
a breeze, the leaning of a golden petal and that
                              presages all—
the hungry root fierce at the balustrade to
                    pull it down,
or in the drier lands a breath of sand blows in
and no one with a broom sweeps it away
                    the harbor silts, meanwhile
sails cease to come, but how invisibly
the work of men is taken from their hands and given
back to the knotted roots and nodding flowers
back to the slithering bushmaster, cobra, asp
back to the golden desert from whence all emerged.
Where did the people go that carved the fallen head
that lies amidst its columns, some lost god?
We talk of atoms and the terrors men have gained
from lasers and great clever new machines
but I look out upon the nodding jungle flower,
the unread hieroglyph upon a brick in rippled sand,
                    and think
the hand that touched it fell away unmarked
and the sand blew and man became the sand,
became the flowers, too, so softly nodding.
The earth makes wraiths of us, prefers to see
the objects we conceived smashed into shards.
Enchantment touches them beyond our hands to hold.
Millennia create beauty, man merely adds his thought
and vanishes into air or pollinates the flower on its
                              stem.

THIS WAS THEIR HISTORY

That cave in the hidden rock face I shall always remember.
One man with a rifle could have held it against a thousand
till his ammunition ran out. There was only one way in—
a fissure up a vertical chimney that made you sweat
even thirty years into the twentieth century.
I came on it by accident sighting the hole
                    and the smoke-blackened overhang
                            of the roof.

Time was they could have watched the wagon trains
                    crawling for miles toward Oregon
                         and later
seen the blue-coats riding and the buffalo go under the grass
                     herd by herd,
a wild people, who preferred these vistas,
          the cold in winter frightful
             and they began to go like the bison.

Here I found only a few flints from the earlier time
               then cartridge cases
               then nothing
               but burnt sticks
               and the horned owl as inheritor.

Starved out, wiped out, whatever happened
             no one had climbed here since.
The distances were the same but now there was a rail line
                    down the valley
          and Herefords had replaced the bison.
This was their history, not skin drums and hoof thunder,
  but a creeping silence and the owl as inheritor.
           Wild voices on the winter northers perhaps,
                        if one listened,

but insubstantial, owl or man, only the wind
keeps singing,
only the yellow dust
knows what little figures trudge the centuries. Only the dust
can whisper in the cyclone's heart: they were all one,
illusion,
wraiths blown from the river bars
wagons, blue-coats, the warriors,
all mine and from me.

Habits little known, little known because of secretive habits:
                    spoken of pandas, spoken of wolverines,
numbers reduced, species decimated, pine martens
scarce since the middle ages, habits solitary.
Page after page my bestiaries dwell on
habits nocturnal, prefers thick forests,
kills everything it meets, the print
grows bolder, wilderness more fierce,
eyes flaming in thickets, panther now
bounds twenty feet, but brought to bay by dogs,
curious about man, alleged dangerous, the tales
confound confusion, but something infests the thicket.
Consult taxonomies, observe footnotes, but there is
a scarcity come upon all these things, there are no wolves
in the wood, and who has seen a musk-ox this year?
                              These volumes are dated.
Of course the cat can spring sixty feet from a cliff-face
but where is the cat?
                    Listen—
all that is little known, all those with habits nocturnal,
all that is soft-footed, crepuscular, all that
                    hangs upside down in caverns
all that is yellow-eyed and can kill in an eye's blink
                    is here, permanently here in me,
                    concentrated in this shadow
                    concentrated in this thicket,
                    soaked up from dead anatomies
                    teleported from anatomized bones.
Do not speak to me of the little known
                    for I know them.
There are eyes in this thicket, my own eyes, I have just
                                        placed
a soft paw at the edge of the street light
          kills everything it meets

advisable now

        most advisable

curious about man

        but not really so curious

          being me. I am constrained to wear claws.

There is no scarcity in me; I absorb scarcity.

           The moment I cross the street light

nothing should be seen

        nothing alarming.

         Let the books go on stating

"habits uncertain"

        let the books say
        "not recently seen"

but there is a paw at the edge of the street light

           eyes in a bush.

What more does one say of scarcity?

        It kills, that is what one can say

          and after a while

even man may be gone.

IN THE TALES TO COME

I have met the echo people, coyotes,
once in my youth, deep in a badland canyon, coming
upon them unaware. They vanished
before I could speak. Esahcawata, Old-man-coyote's people
quick of foot, hunted by all, surviving
traps and poison bait, surviving
where the great wolves have vanished, admirable
tricksters in an endless war. I would have spoken
peace, but my kind know it not. They did well
not to trust me—the trap-shy scurriers at midnight.
Their songs are few now. They live by the thoughts
of Esahcawata and no other thinking is
                              possible for them.
Their songs echo the wind. They are echo people
                                but all
under the sky are echoers and the millennia listen
                           and are silent.
It will be so with us. I have remembered
all my life how fast they scampered. We the laughers
do not understand fear because of our numbers
                        and when we vanish
no one will tell stories about our cleverness, the night wind
will not long echo laughter for Old-man, the trickster
married the whirlwind and myth will have us
as part of the singular spinning of a dust-devil
on a dry prairie. They are the echoers, we
a jumble of leaves and dust
quickly gone by. Lovers of form we will be formless
in the tales to come.

STAR WITH A SECRET

Older than time the Jodrell Bank pulsar 1953
ticks without running down, is hanging
in constellation Cygnus, one thousand
light years away in a cold, cool timelessness,
a cave of blue having seemingly
outlasted the present universe, a survivor
of the universe before. We cannot reach it.
Jodrell Bank and the great cup at Arecibo
can only count its heart beat and know
it is not like men or anything mortal, even stars
in the present universe. If immortality
is to outlast two universes collapsing inward,
                           and their renewal,
then this creature in the constellation Cygnus
is the terrible eye of all the past, surveying
ruin undreamt of, fixed on universes yet to be.
               Man, a brief flicker between two darknesses,
               has found him out in the blue
               inscrutable cavern of fire, but no one
dares ask or be answered, in human terms
how many times the play has been repeated. It is a star
with a secret unyielded, not to the finite,
               nor reveals what hand placed it,
                      in the cool impenetrable cave.

FLY FALCON

All of the falcon kind, the hard travelling
                     talon-clawed ones
that for so many years I have seen
go over Hawk Mountain on thousand-mile journeys—
at heart I go with them, but I also travel
with the fluttering Monarch butterflies,
toss on gales lost at sea, or cross the Gulf
                     with humming birds.
You think this impossible? not with the mind's eye
                          my friend
                   the ever widening eye
of the living world, the eye that someday
will see all as one, the eye of the hurricane,
                       the eye
at the heart of the galaxy with the spinning
                   arms of the suns about it.
Fly falcon, fly Monarch, fly gull
                   and you in the invisible night-tiger's eye

going somewhere in reed grass. I am there
padding softly with you, fly albatross
that sleeps on the Cape Horn winds. We are all
the terrible eye that sees the galaxy,
                             we make it real.
Without us multiplied, what really exists?
Fly falcon, stare tiger in the night grass,
stare that the universe may find itself living
beyond the immortal fires.

TWO HOURS FROM NOW

Two hours from now there will be dawn
in the place of my childhood, light in the room,
but another will turn slowly with sleep-ridden eyes,
                              not knowing
the continuity of flesh or what lingers
in the wisps of night as the high plains sunlight
touches the window, or the little walk where my father
used to sit with the papers on Sunday. Only I
in this eastern city remember a brief while
and then go my own ways knowing no one
can put two things together. The old house, I suppose,
insentient, calm, does not remember, nor its inhabitants,
or the quarter lost under the front porch, or the room
                              in which I wept from a quarrel
or the gas stove in the kitchen by which I studied.
                              Mother is gone,
Father sleeps on a hilltop in another town.
                    We were all lonely.
I had no brothers. I have no children. Why do I write
                    to myself as
                    dawn is breaking
                    two thousand miles away?
Nothing will be solved. The house does not remember,
                    nor the dead, nor will the window curtain waver.
I have followed the dawn to no purpose, there are only
    the paws
of a lost puppy imprinted in the cement of the sidewalk.
I, the living ghost, stare at them across two thousand miles
                              and do not speak.
There is also a toy boat still hidden in the attic.

BEAU

Beau is gone now,
the huge black poodle
who, when I visited his owners,
always used to wave his yellow food dish
happily from the doorway and bark his welcome
or lie beside my bed in the morning.
This afternoon on the patio
his diminutive challenger the chipmunk
who used to set Beau wild
whistled dispute from the wall
but there was only silence.
I think even the chipmunk was abashed.
They had had a long rivalry and now silence
had fallen. A lily nodded gently
on its stem and I
went to my room where Beau
would never again turn three times around
and subside with a patient sigh while I wrote.
I am not a philosopher. I merely know
everything good has an end. I hope Beau
left without having learned this.
Yesterday his girl playmate from up the road
came by slowly, having come before.
How does one explain this to animals: that after a while
there are none of us left: no shadows, no voice, no odor.
One cannot even show a picture.
She goes away silently up the track.
She does not understand the world's absences.
Looking at the empty rug by my bed,
neither do I.

MOONSHINER'S THICKET

Just now because of a phrase in a newspaper
"the Missouri breaks"
I remembered the frozen river
and the willow stands on the islands
young red willows all vertical and leafless in the snow
till you were made dizzy
                        and had to look at the path above them
zigzagging to the top of the bluffs.
It was moonshiner's country then.
One had to be careful,
but on that day there was only
the frozen river and the trail staggering upward
the wind stinging one's eyes.
A reflex, I guess,
but my eyes still sting reading the phrase.
I remember climbing the bluff but to where?
Headed to where in that dead winter?
I no longer remember topping the bluff
I remember just the trail
and the willow breaks in the white snow.
My eyes water a little
I presume I made it over the rise
and came finally after some years
to this room I inhabit.
It is strange to remember no more, as though life,
the meaningful part of it,
had been lost following a zigzag
out of a moonshiner's thicket.
There was not even the glimpse of a far horizon.

A HIDER'S WORLD

Once in my callous evil youth I saw a bittern
take two steps in the reeds of a swamp thus ceasing
to be a reed. Then it straightened again, pointed up its bill
                                   and I
lost it or pretended to. My companion did not see it,
it was a reed again and I chose to lose it.
                         Since then
I am bittern-minded, try to keep my own place in the reeds
                                   not engage
overmuch in the world. Storms go over the marsh
                       of the cities.
I have feet in the mud, eyes like the brown water,
drench inconspicuously, have survived

years in the city jungle, crossed streets to avoid conflict
but the bitterns
must have had a purpose, pointing beaks at the sky.
Genes informed them
to act like reeds and breed other reed actors
with pointed beaks upturned. I
have survived the disguise of a teacher,
dusted my clothing with chalk, spoken
to the unlistening, but for what, I want to know
now that it is ending. Why does a bittern stand
so successfully on one leg? Is this the purpose
he was formed for and as for me, dusted with chalk,
eyes not to be seen on a dark night, what was the
purpose
engendered
in me? To love, and conceal it all of my life
like the bittern
trying to be a reed? We are necessary failures, bird,
necessary to keep something alive that the time
is not ripe for.
Remain with your camouflage, bittern, but someday
they will find
an old coat in the city, somebody wearing it who loved
everything in hiding and being
just itself. The man will be drenched and muddy and
will certainly
be disposed of, as long ago it had been my intention with the
bittern
on the day I lost my youth and laid the rifle
quietly aside for the sake of hiders. That, I think,
has been my purpose, a hider's world.

THE BUZZARDS

The air on a hot day came up out of the dark chasm, cool
as the wind off the ice front that had left
a stream in the canyon, pines on the cliffside. It took me
                    a good while to learn
I could always find buzzards there
wheeling on the rising draft with that grace
that belied their occupation, till they
were flecks in the sky. I only found them once
on the ground above the chasm, mysterious, silent,
like an undertakers' convention without a cadaver
unless it was I they were measuring but did not want
to be obvious behind such clairvoyant vision, so they turned
                          and huddled,
thirty perhaps, but it struck me, though big as turkeys,
they were not frightened. I could be dealt with
all in good time like ground things, and they continued
their deliberations ignoring me; I am not
              a stick-throwing person.
It left me with a fey sense of time disorganized,
                         the ice just gone
a trifle of ten thousand years, the pines intermediate,
                      the buzzards—
who knows when a buzzard comes except on updrafts, and I
parked below on the roadside. The world is a jumble really
                  and I a man
quite recent, trying to remember the ice-caves
                    we huddled under
worshipping a mother carved in mammoth ivory, not knowing
the way we had come, but feeling always the clairvoyant eyes
                    of the buzzards
still following our trail across immeasurable tundras.

THE CACTI ARE NEUTRAL

The cacti are neutral but aware of the world
                              in a dreamer's fashion.
I have raised them for years, attended their few wants
a little soil, water at rare intervals, these and the sun.
They have stabbed me at times quite impartially for misjudging
the distances they choose to keep, not really trusting
anything but small owls and trade rats. They are
another planet's offspring, or better say, the desert's world.
Why should they care if their thorns bite?
                              It is no apparent matter
if they live or die, dreaming dark soundless dreams
of a life not our life, dreaming as one might suspect
a desert to dream, without conceivable definition,
                                        preferring
only to hold distance with thorns, not conscious
even of the distance but implying
the dream center must be kept inviolate for juices
                                        and thorns
in themselves precious for reasons that the mind's
incalculable distances and tangential reasoning
here fail at completely. Perhaps it is thus in the end
                                        that the dead
withdraw to the bitter sources of the Holy Land
and find comfort in sharp nails, harsh wood and a crown
thorn-woven for penitence. I make the analogy dubiously
        wondering why mankind and the desert
                share this ultimate passion for thorns unless flesh
                is always a thing to be raked.

MARS

Two hundred million miles and instructions are
                                        given,
                        the light at morning
is photographed in pink and wafted
to a room on earth. The desert is rust-red,
                        the stones lie
as our stones, the water courses are dry,
                        the temperatures
fall in the freezing nights, rise in the blazing day,
                        a planet
without men, without leaves,
                        a pitiless loneliness
                where only a space probe
turns a merciless
mechanical eye on the horizon.
                        How little room in the universe
is accorded life. For every yearning there is
an abandoned rivulet, for every sorrow
a drifting dust veil, and, worst of all, for loneliness
                                        not even
evidence of an abandoned well. The sand lifts and blows
and has, for a billion years,
never known sentience, nor a voice crying
to another voice. No eye till this moment
has seen color in this world. It is now transmitted
                                        elsewhere.
                        Here is the void where tears
by no means known to man can fall, and yet
                        two hundred million
miles away they fall for those unborn, unused, reactivated
by the unrolling film that prints
light where no eye exists.

HOPE TO SEE MORNING

Men always live on the sides of Vesuvius, mountains in Turkey,
Guatemala, Krakatoa, the San Andreas fault, or to perish
at Herculaneum in the midst of business,
                                          or Pompeii at siesta—
small people who trusted the earth, the gods, something
to continue and it did, but between, those unspeakable periods
                                          when nothing
arose but smoking vapors, sulphur and the
seas' withdrawal that Pliny records leaving beasts
                              on the shore,
                              the ash-rain falling.

Knossus or Zakros, the lives taken
idly as fruit plucked from a branch
who has a word for them? the lost lovers,
the old and wise under the oil lamps, hearing
the dreadful knocking in the earth.

We, the moderns, knowledgeable, but children still
in these matters, build and love in the same fashion.
Tide, tremor and hurricane overcome us but to whom
do we make obeisance now, to whom
address ourselves?
                    If the deities were remorseless
is not the shifting of strata more so?
No. I once saw two crosses placed at a ruin and assumed
someone felt gratitude though the earth had shuddered
                                          frightfully in that place.

I did not laugh. I departed in silence and asked
grace of the destroyer—being a man and humble
before winds, temblors, and all things that strike
                              out of season
be they gods possessed, or forces unknown, equally driven
out of human orbit. Make the sign and hope to see morning.

Nothing has changed since the shrines boiled in the mud
                                        at Herculaneum.
Men return and the ring of fire may be brooding even now
                        like a scorpion curled in the hearthstone.

MAN IN THE LONG TERM

"Too far did I fly into the future: a horror seized me,"
thus spoke Nietzsche searching his madness.
                              Here on the sands at evening
following my own tenuous and extended shadow as it lengthens
                              beyond the sunset
I have thought this thin projection of myself
might reach another dimension no one of this age frequents.
The horror is here, not there, perhaps Nietzsche
                              overestimated his journey by centuries,
for beyond as I follow the lengthening shadow
                    the sand lifts and blows, old towers,
the power carriers, lean askew in the wind, bits of wire
not totally corroded hang like moss from the metal poles
                              and the poles themselves
rust, the insulators are
                    broken, everything is broken
in the wind, the intolerable wind,
                              sand engulfs
                              everything
the giant pipes coming up from the sea
                              last efforts,
beautiful technology,
                    the enormous calculations
expended for nothing.
                    Man in the long term
                    no more than an animal
can fight the sly earth.
                    Deserts creep
                              poles shift
                    continents slide like dinner plates
                              under our feet.
I wonder what final messages
                    in fear or wisdom
what muttered static

troubled the listeners
                              the video screens
going finally dark.
                    Did someone desperate
lift his searching binoculars skyward and in despair
hurl them down the embankment?
                              The sound is instantly gone.
                              There is no horror here,
                                             none.
We enlarge ourselves beyond nature to see horror.
                    Here on these present sands where my shadow
runs a long way out into the future is a small bird.
He is rare now for no visible reason—
                    like man fits many possible environments.
Still, he is rare for no
                    ascertainable reason,
content, it seems, with his small song subsiding now forever
into the voice of the wind.
                    Man has not destroyed him. He has simply
reached the length of his shadow. He is going quietly
                              singing this small song to join
the winds' voices, just as forward by some millennia
                    the crash of a field glass rolling
marks the end of man.
                    There is no horror here, only the limitations
of the wise earth.

THE BLACK SNAKE

The snake came through the boards of the old bridge
black, glistening, innocent as before the Fall
                                    and my wife,
as befits women, saw him first and screamed.
All he wanted was to bask in the sun and I would wager
the whole Biblical story came from a similar imputation
                                    of the wrong motives
                        and maybe
irritation on the snake's part afterward.
                        I wouldn't blame him
                                for stirring things up a little
                                after being screamed at, so he
on the old bridge in Ohio oozed legless and shining
into a crack and no persuasion would bring him out.
But the place was a fragment of lost Eden
—old boards, no travellers, a clear stream in limestone, fish
that walked on the bottom with fins as though thinking
of coming out and starting things all over again. I could sit
by the hour, legs dangling, and dream worlds not made and
                                                    creatures
all potential, but the black snake
never came back nor whispered to anybody.
Time stopped there and remained Eden. I think I was the only
                                                    creature
half regretful, but not enough to pick an apple in the
                                silent orchard.

THE LITTLE TREASURES

All spilled on the outwash fan where the glacial stream
                              finally subsided—
the pebbles that rattled downward in the mountain torrents—
a polished flint from the hand that dropped it
                    ten thousand years ago.
                    Where is the hand now?
                    In what language
                    is the flint remembered?
They are both lost on the air but the blade that fits
                              my forefinger
is it glad that its perfection is still admired?

I huddle over these little treasures
                    one, a round stone abraded
                         by someone knocking
                    a bit of the inanimate into human shape.
On this great strewn gravel bed of the world
how wonderful it seems to be picking it over
just as on the first morning
                    when a man wandered up from the sea.
Everything is glistening, rain-washed.
I am alone, there is still ice high in the Sierras
                    waiting to come down.
I am very vulnerable here among the boulders of quartzite
              and have forgotten much learning
                 remembering only how it will be beyond us
                    when the ice begins to move.
I have spent the whole day splitting pebbles and forgetting
why I came here or if I might be the first man coming
                    into his heritage
                    or the final one
                              departing.
There is little difference. We have moved only a few stones
                                        and the ice
         can be seen far up on the mountain.

This day I have huddled over the little treasures.
They fill my mind.
I know now what impulse created the Olmec heads
                              Mayan stelae and Machu Picchu.
The stone will survive us. Like the Old Ones I have left
                              a shaped stone in the gravel.
It is all my knowledge. It will lie there when no one
                              interprets these words.
It will lie there when earth's perturbed orbit
                              drifts toward the final dark.
My stone will stretch the shadow of the last evening.
For what else have stones been shaped
but to prolong the human presence and to say
                              soundlessly in lost tongues:
        We loved the earth
                      but could not stay?
We it was and not the immortals
            who shaped the stones.

THE EYE DETACHED

The far reach of the void, the eye
detached from the eye begins to haunt us, seeing
across two hundred million miles rock shadows
form the illusion of letters, seeing
things without meaning there, but here
electronically translated into dust clouds
wandering the eternal waste, the place
                              where man
would be most lonely he must needs create
a far laboratory to engender one friendly microbe
                              if such do exist.
O Martian day lit by the black light of no eyes,
blind craters, blinkless sockets gazing
where no rain falls, here
nothing has died, been born, since yesterday's
                              four billion years. The universe
is not for man, it is
itself, out there the star stuff is wrenched free
                        it does not seed
reproduce, devour, it is and is only.
The letter on the broken rock is the mind's mockery.
                              Go up among
high rocks where clouds and hailstones
stream over nothing. Be content
with chuckling irreverent ravens, see, if at all,
with a newt's beaded eye, let orange lichens grow
upon your forehead, all firsts of things, but then brush off
raven and newt and lichen, be
as earth will be sometime when a far probe
drops in the mountains and its lens discerns
where light once entered and a creature laughed
laughed at its own minute far-travelling eye and laughed
once for the ungrieved solitudes of Mars and once
for heartbreak Earth, so loved, so multitudinously
extinct.

MY FACE BENEATH THE SKIN

Habits elusive, seldom seen by day, dens
                    with two entrances
could be fox, badger, jackal, also me
except so often flight-hatch filled with stones.
                I slink
as best I can, field to field, hedgerow to hedgerow
increasingly under wires, threatened by poison bait,
thorn trees mostly gone, coverts filled with fence wire
                         taking over.
You think I do not know, being garbed in cloth,
                           what happens here?
Whose skin is caught on barbs, whose belly bloats with poison?
Listen, I have been running since I first ventured
                from a den—
a house long, long forgot, slung stones in alleys
                  against roving gangs,
fought in the sunflower forests of dead creek beds
                  always alone,
last of a solitary human litter, I
should lift this rifle now against all who ran
and huddled with me, furred or feathered
breathing quick breaths, sometimes their last, in corn rows or
crouched in fading range grass, oh no
my face beneath the skin is their face, teeth the same.
                        Down to this very day
            I board the local as in camouflage
for jungle warfare, know the city as I once knew hedgerows,
                  walk in the subway
                  as in sunflower thickets.
Vietnams are everywhere. I have survived,
grow old, see not so well, no longer trust a burrow,
prefer the open when the hunt is on, gain little,
                know the end,
but lurk like the last fox, ears lifted,
his earths all blocked with stones, but curious

watching the hounds come baying down the field.
I know where I will fall, here in the open cornered,
escapes all closed, this human mask torn off for just
one lifetime's solitary bite. We live under illusion always
no escape route has two exits, but one only
whether for badger, fox or man. Hold in the corner, meet
the running hounds with what was given you at birth
teeth, teeth, and then alone to see
the whole vast pageant of the stars wink out.

NIGHT IS OUR LORD

First voice   They left flowers in the tomb's darkness;
       they were men like us
       uncertain, wistful,
       believing, not believing,
       conscious that no one came back, conscious
       of shades at nightfall, bearing guilt, bearing all
       the living endure before the accusing dead.

Second voice Say how it was we made a gold mask
           for the dissolving features,
       how we erected
       the many-chambered tomb, incised
       the hieroglyphs, addressed Osiris, painted
             the coffin texts—
       we, mortal, we whose bones are lost now,
       we whom night has enfolded.
       We left our king with the first dagger of iron and
              the hooded cobra
       guarding his forehead.
       It was for him alone that we labored
       at the wrought stone.
       It was for each of us and all
       who came after, fearing the night.
       He was our king, the god whom the sun had favored.

First voice   Now we
       we leave flowers still in the tomb's darkness
       and the heavy cross
       replaces the hooded uraeus.
       Iron is common, our rulers are not gods
       to find for us a way
       through the swamps of Nilus.
       How should we speak of this
       before the indifferent stars?

Everything has been tried. We leave you
as the dead were once left
with an offering of corn flowers.
Iron will not serve, nor arrows,
then perhaps flowers. It is true they wilt,
but they the sun has once favored.
Deny it not
at the doorway of the tomb.
Much has passed away but not this.
Lay the flowers and go, saying simply:
He was ours upon whom the sun once rested.
The cobra will not strike,
the drawn bow cannot defend him.
Night is our lord but we bend our necks stubbornly.

DRUID BORN

"I was druid born," said the poet, "I was druid born
                              and all things
spoken by leaves and tree roots are manifest to me.
                        I know the very tree
that split Arthur's rock, when he drew Excalibur.
It still lives in a lone glen, birds speaking its prophecies
on moonlit nights. Can you equal,
you to whom sciences are read, what was spoken of destiny
by the helmed man?"
            "That the world has changed, yes," I countered.
"Arthur would have known, Merlin confirmed it—
wings in the air, the armor-plate thicker,
chain mail abandoned—these the helmed man being wise
would have foreseen and the cross-hilted sword
flung at last to the arm in the freezing water.
                        It rusts in oblivion now
                              but the wars
are as always, this, too, would not surprise him
                  who knew the violence of wounds
and the equal violence of gods—their stone heads leering
                        or finally cast down
faceless in grass."
            I will tell you the least things, I, not a druid.
Last evening I saw a small rabbit peer from a bush
                        beside a thruway.
I saw a bat taking insects, swooping behind a signboard.
                              I saw
a snake creeping on a lilac bush in black coils
                  whisper in sibilants what was
                        manifest to him;
namely, that the armor
would finally pass and a great quiet
fall on the smoldering world, a quiet of remaining leaves
                        and small things,
                  the iron and the flint being stilled.

He whispered no more, history having ended. Ask me
never beyond man, the memory-carrier.
   "I am druid born," said the poet. "I speak not
when oaks refuse and birds grow quiet as before a storm."
   "Well then, poet," I said, "by science and necromancy,
by the interrogation of trees and serpents
     we have come to where history ends.
It was forecast when the dripping
    upthrust arm
received Excalibur. There was enacted the concealed
      final prophecy
man-made, in the surety that the seer Merlin
of all men knew, but put off in disguised fashion
     muffling the thunder overhead,
silently awaiting the death sounds of an age."
    So the poet druid born
and I, the uncertain scribe, waited as one by the oak
     at midnight.
This I know: there were no birds anywhere in its branches.

st to swallow one living creature—I could feel
                              in the hot sun
e numbness creep up my toes and ankles, beckoning.

he place was a hole into time, a blue eye of
                    smiling deception
                    cruel and yet innocent, because
ulls were its only familiars in the depths, its eye
e blue of drowned eyes; it had once known
                    ice caverns that had trapped mammoth.
drew back and the eye continued to follow me
                         with its beckoning coolness
                         but I saw it was blind
 time is blind, forgetting, in the millennia, the anguish
                    that lies there in the depths
                    of the blue bottomless water,
ndling the polished bone and waiting insatiable, smiling
                         for more eras to pass that these
ueer little animate forms might be restfully enfolded.

THE BLUE EYE

The rock quarry by the gray walls of the state penite
was abandoned, and the older youths swam there
                              on hot days.
It had the coldest, bluest water imaginable
                    and the cliff behind it
was the locked gravel of a far-past ice sheet
                              something fading
into a remote vista of giant tossing horns and tusks,
                        man utterly absent.

I stripped once there alone and waded out, but a fear
                              struck me.
After a short way the place was bottomless
                    the crepitations of the cold
crept over my body even as I stood in the sun.
                        No one would hear my cries
                        and I, momentarily clairvoy
felt the cold mount upward grasping for a victim,
          a cold waiting for two hundred thousand

DREAMED IN A DARK MILLENNIUM

Dreamed in a dark millennium I did not live
in human time, but rather was a crawling landscape of eons,
boulders gouged out, great canyons scarred my face,
mesas of thought were heaped on me by winds,
and all that time amidst light, darkness, desert rains,
I lived and dreamed some planetary dream,
myself, old earth-father, had devised, indifferent to life
stiff-jointed mostly, in the gully fans and washes.

Who's to care what troubles a continental face?
Ice, saber teeth, or mammoth tusks, they melt or drop
and are forgotten while the face lives on, primordial
cross-hatched, seamed in distorted strata, but somehow young
                                    and smiling still
about some work, some dream. Great God
who'd wish in a single night to penetrate
the mighty caverns of the intellect and find
such ruin prized there, but such building too,
stone laid on stone to heave a mountain up and then to place
some yellow-eyed and cloudy-coated leopard
high on the cliffs to rule amidst the blizzards.
                                    Beauty then
out of the stones and slashes, and, just at the edge
                      of morning, light.
Stretched in my bed, my giant continental bed, I sighed,
having glimpsed man, some way within myself, and wept,
wept for what it was he strove, for what he lost,
                      could not attain, wept
in the cold morning, joyed again to live, in the half light
                      before the daylight came.

THE FUNGUS BED

Fungi with names unknown
spring up in the wet October nights
like thoughts in a dying brain
morbidly purple some of them
or pale as Indian pipe in the woods,
starred, and the squirrels eat them
and then there are the little silver puff balls
giving off their spores in the rain
                              little brown specks
that vanish like thoughts to emerge
in another century when the time is ripe.
                  A yard filled with damp and the long rains
heaves up with ghosts when everything
is dying—an old brain, I think,
does that task also in the sleepless nights,
turning its mulch, its ashes, milkweed down
rotted for decades in its own peculiar autumn.
Pods rattle, mycelia creep in the neuron beds
                       and breed up things
a squirrel might eat, or pale elusive spores
blow for a last time in the uncertain gusts
of fading memory, girls' faces with no names attached
met in another autumn, all farewells too late spoken
by one man in his sleep. Still, branches tap the window
                     what moves in the earth outside
is working here—October's ruin, but the brain
turns its dead leaves to use, glowing like unseen fire-worms
                              where I gaze
sleepless, down one long dark forever
               and put out my hand
                    helpless upon a pillow's substance,
                    I, who once held so much.

NO PLACE FOR BOY OR BADGER

Osage apples, great red roots guarded the roadside,
in hidden corners made homes for foxes, woodchucks
this within my lifetime and now at long intervals
I come there and walk the straight streets
                    through the endless suburbs
                            wondering
what became of the snagged impermeable roots—
they used dynamite—the foxes are gone—there is
no place for boy or badger to hide in the hedgerows.
Everything is lawns, suburbia, split-level houses.
There is not one bush, one jagged root intertwined
no milkweed pods in autumn, no tiger swallowtails floating.
This in one generation, the wild land played upon.
Now I am old and the smooth lawns and
                        the smooth faces
do not please me. I played hide and seek here
with comrades and little girls. I suppose
in the nights badgers and foxes took over for us.
What was it all for, where are we now?
I know of only one man who limps away on a stick.
I suppose the dynamite got the foxes.
                        What was it all for? The long green
golf courses, the fenced-in swimming pools of
                        the wealthy?
Did some good come from the dead foxes, dead roots,
dead men? Somewhere we must be mentioned.
Then mention it here, like the last of a
                        beaten army,
not with anger, mention it that we in playtime
may be remembered, even the delicate wings
                of the butterflies must not be lost.

AND WE WEPT, EACH ONE

In the glow of the lamp, darkness, the farseen,
                          never forgotten
darkness of childhood, things held on the walls, time
at bay here, held, do you understand,
like a castle with banners, laces encircling
                    her mother's face,
candles, the polished brass in the kitchen
                        immortal, and I
smile, as at a light seen twenty miles away through
                             a snow flurry and say gently
there is Laddie, there is Snippet, in the photograph safe
                          forever
                for as long as we, the living,
                keep them inviolate.
                        But the heart
ticks, ticks like the clock in the kitchen.
                  We are holding
an outpost in time.
                God help me there are circumstances
when I
          no longer can see clearly
              the light in the evening, the old plates
                    of the ancestors
close in their brackets. What will become of us
when the clock stops or the first plate falls and smashes
                      on the floor?
Dear Lady, they knew this when one's belongings,
magical even then, were placed in sewn bags that the dead
                      were given under the cromlech.
Kings had their longships, brooches and their favorite swords;
in Greece the lost book scroll of the philosopher.
When have men stopped time? But tonight in a house
                    not my house

and terror at my throat, I turned my face to the lamp
and said:
Let us play as if this were forever. Let us imagine
like children.
And we wept, each one, for the dead, and imagined
we were not powerless but held a castle inviolate
bravely with banners.

LONDON: A MEMORY

Happy, the happy swallows take to air
weaving a dance above crushed stone and iron.
Urban renewal they neither know nor care
only the rusted iron, the fallen fence
only time pulverized, a half-city fallen
joys the glad heart as if mad Spitfires spun and wheeled
over a still ghostly burning London.

I cannot hear their twitters through impervious glass
here on the heights of this upthrust hotel
but by the massive window, in the sinking sun,
as if for me alone,
they touch wings, fall away, return and flash
a moment in the dying light, red-black, a miniature
of that sky war so long since done.

I look into the field of blasted iron, but one bird darts
out of his thirty fellows and drives straight
toward me and my concerns, a harbinger
out of that time now past, the rakish wings, forked tail
race up the last red of the burning town, the eye
looks at me straight and dances off again,
so do they all, happy, the happy swallows think we're done,
gone with the night, rusted iron, old engines, old defeats.

Something within me joins their furious revel—
no steel tomorrow, no lime-mixers churning, no tall columns
rising,
only the clover come, only the grass to cover
what birds remember if they do remember.
The sun is speckled with their brief wild dance;
my heart is wilder from their one swift glance.
Happy, the happy swallows have passed on.
Crashed Heinkels, Spitfires rust, our day sinks with the sun.

SOMEWHERE BEYOND THE PAWNSHOPS

They say that rats always leave a sinking ship.
                They say that after a certain age
the gray cells, neurons, axons, whoever they are sneak down
                        trembling ladders
in the brain's midcenter, carpetbaggers loaded
                with a lifetime's dreams.
They say after a drink of whiskey
           a million of their little lights blink out
           leaving the decks bare.
In the raw mornings I can feel them missing,
wonder about that girl they were supposed to have charge of—
                    was it Emily or Rose?
Her face is leached, unrecognizable. I told her
                I distinctly told her
I would remember forever, and I would—
              but the crew is slowly deserting
carrying picture frames they have no right to.

Where in hell do they market such stocks in dockland,
what pawnshops?
Who wants the face of a dead girl? What's the price, mister?
Who wants the bastard I fought back and forth
                across the steel rails
                until he fell
and looked up once before the night swallowed him?
              Who buys pictures like that
              or the crying sounds
              behind a locked door forever
              closed to me now?
Listen, I know this is getting to be a tub.
The paint's gone, there's salt bilge in the scuppers,
the glad words don't come readily.
              In the night I feel things leaving
              I was sworn to keep.

Get this carcass out to sea, Mr. Mate.
We're sailing to where they can't climb out anymore.
The plates are scaling through. Never mind the paint.
Old iron has its uses, there are new maps
                        and pictures in it.
On my face, too. That's the last place
                        you can find your memories.
There's a door somewhere beyond the pawnshops.
Take her out, mister, till the last damn synapse goes.
Head her into tomorrow's morning.
We've got the last treasure—
                It's today.
Don't search the pawnshops.
Something hurts in here, mister.
Take her out, let the rats run with their
                little bags of loot.
There's something ahead.
It's spare yards and seas with a long green roll now.
Jettison, Mr. Mate, jettison and consult my face.
Rose, Emily, they're long gone.
The next sea will be sufficient.
There was always too much crew.

SAY THAT THE GIFT WAS GIVEN

Say that the gift was given long ago—
the little cat that by the roadside cried so piteously
till lifted up and saved and that was love;
say that it takes all forms out of some human center
                              heartbreak knows—

love given to serpents, to great clouded leopards moving
in snowstorms, and there is love in snowflakes, crystals, too.
So much love that catalogues must be kept by bees
out of the odors of the springtime grass,
and there is love in atoms that makes sapphires in the dark.

Only remember when you give such love
to mountain freshets or to trees that fall
you give yourself past every human shape
and nothing is recallable—it stays,
cries in the heart with winter and old age.
A girl's eyes are a girl's and once seen are forever.

So does the falcon perching, or the water ouzel
walking beneath waterfalls and icy torrents
perceive the great rain of the world go past
and if they see that way, so must the lover.

THE DEER

Along the public road but deep enough in the glade
so that everything was
                    glancing, flickering,
                dappled with sunlight,
the buck deer stepped out suddenly on the path and we met.

He was too innocent to savor fear
or the terror that followed him.
He had young proud horns and was the most alive
of anything I have ever met in the wood.
He raised his ears gravely before me as though
                    he had heard
                for the first time
a sound from the dark behind him
                  unpronounced, undefined.

"You do this twice and you won't live the season out,"
I told him there at the forest's edge, but he only
looked at me mildly
              ruminating
              considering
the wraith from the forest floor
suddenly confronting him.

Perhaps he has not seen me as a man, I thought,
but as an emanation, a creature of warning.

Slowly he drew back and in the glade
                        among leaf patterns
vanished softly where a moment before
the dappled delicate head had proudly
lowered its budding antlers.

This is the nearest I have ever stood to the wild.
The place lies there still just beyond the high road.
I have never seen him since.
I it was who brought him the word
                        never till then defined—
          death.

I must have smelled of it like pine smoke.
It is in the clothes of men
in their voices from which everything flees.
I was the messenger though I tried to whisper discreetly.
He made his own definition
and survived, I hope for a time he survived
the word of which I smelled like a forest burning.

WHY DOES THE COLD SO HAUNT US?

Why does the cold so haunt us—the great ice
                              receding and advancing
                        all in mystery?
The interglacial summers helped man live
                        but since he's grown
conscious of what once shared his world
                              and by its locked-up seas allowed
his intercontinental march across dry shelves
before an oar had dipped into a wave, before a star
                              had beckoned.
Today we trace the ice, we learn the temperate zone
                              once held
gigantic elephants and roving beasts
that traveled on the flanks of summer snow.

They are all gone and man a remnant here
left by the ice that will march back again.
We are things forgotten when the ice withdrew,
                        and meant to perish really,
but the ice forgot, and somehow from the ice-streams
                              we survived
—a tough ill-mannered beast, outthinking all the rest.

There's just one thing: whatever made us never taught
how to outthink ourselves. That will be needed when
                              the fifth
of those great rhythms moves its dragon limbs
and thrusts against a billion-bodied huddled mass
no longer fit to drift and follow
                        the trails the reindeer took
                        between the closing crystal corridors.
I think ten thousand years ago the frost forgot
its muddy unexterminated children.
They're like the ice, they spread. I think the fifth
                              great snow will not forget;

I think no scurrying will help our cause. Our destined bones
                                                    will line
old gravel pits. Mammoth or saber-tooth or man,
                there'll be no difference then.
                Our interglacial summer passes quickly on.

THE GREAT QUEENS DIE

That year there were more of them than usual.
                              Sphex wasps,
                                  digging
their little cratered city close together.
I watched them through late summer into the pale
September sun. The great queens with their
                              tiger faces
live a month, maybe a little more, the males
two weeks among the flowers—all is adjusted, timed
to the locusts' pattern that the females prey upon
for food they never touch, the larval food
down in the city's depths.
                              But, alas, that city—
that swarming hillside with its busy wings—
is only summer in its going. The great queens die off
deep in the last crater or asleep upon a flower.
All is ended, save I alone
watch a lost queen slowly circling
                              over the pitted ground
                                  of her own digging.
She, like the last space ship above a ruined world
Circles twice more, then darts off headlong as if beyond
                              the universe
another city waited. I alone in the pale sun
am touched by winter, red leaves and the wind
sifting its elements by abandoned doorways.
I alone am ignorant of resurrection
but deep within the city's sleeping heart
the larvae of great queens dream of another summer
                              that to me
will never, never come—
                    not to me ever, pale in this final sun.

RATTLESNAKE

A spirit flowing downward over rocks' excrescences
finding
his way through crevices, the darting tongue
sensing an obstacle in some inhuman
informative way, goes as the mind goes,
like water seeking its level, but pausing, considering
as if a great thought toyed with a poem or the philosophy
that shaped a universe. I have watched him
coiled asleep, the spade-shaped head
with its vial of poison, not frightening, merely practical
the world being the world, the sun warm
the body to be nourished by the death-seeking face
mottled, pitted and beautiful
to those fitted by nature to see
the grandeur of mesas and to appreciate
that in this world, at least, the heat-sensing
blood-follower in the rock channel has his
reasons,
as we, more nebulous, less defined by the black border,
have our own, but may tolerate and be
the better for the chill of this frost in the afternoon
sunlight.

THE DOLL HOUSE

Given to me long ago by a master carpenter now dead
the old Victorian house sits on a table in my study.
There are bookcases in the living room and a lovely small lady
rocks in an equally small chair, before the fireplace.
A cat drowses on the rug, a clock holds tea-time forever.

I have been out many winters in storms and leaves falling,
seen trees topple, brawled with my kind in the world
                              but now
the old house seems my only possession, the books my books,
                                        and I peer
through the bay window at the ageless lady and wish to tap
                                        on the glass.
I have waited too long. I cannot enter that serenity,
cannot reduce to the proper size, nor stroke the cat.
                              The master carpenter in irony
saw what would happen to me in the years coming.

The front doors fit perfectly, they can be opened,
                              but to what avail?
The lady will not arise; the clock will never pass tea-time
even though moonlight falls on the floor.
                              I touch with an aging finger
what I will never possess. When I am gone who will
                              care for the house,
the library, or the clock set for tea-time? Who will protect
the drowsing cat by the fireplace? Who will whisper
                              brokenly
to the ageless lady: I love you, but I waited too long.
                              I grew up.

Does a grown man draw inward and become
      the little clockwork figure he would wish to be?
        Bow to the ageless lady,
        pour the tea and say
        "We are alone. The front door is closed forever.
        I have just come in.
        There is no outside.
        I have abolished it."

HOW BRIEF UPON THE WIND

Crossed tusks, the huge teeth mineralized
in bog iron, mastodons from the drift ice—
who knows what happened once when rivers overflowed,
                              when muskeg trapped
the last great giants of the Pleistocene?
                    Now the wild oak
strews acorns here. The forest trails are dim and
                        nothing trumpets
even far-off the longings of these beasts; their voices died—
lost on the winds of ten millennia ago. Not pride,
                        not strength,
not elephantine wisdom were sufficient. They are gone.
There is a silence in the forest aisles, a silence
where the dropped boulders of the continental drift
denote the extreme limit of the ice, a dripping
in little buried pools—all else is featureless.
                        How will it be
with man, I wonder, in the time when he
grows scarce as the pacing cats once did and the last bogs
                        yield up
a few fantastic skulls with root hairs probing
cold sockets that once saw what doom approached?
                        Black bog iron covers
what happened then and now begins enveloping
what is to be. I think that man will rust as
                        readily
into oblivion as elephants. It is hard to pity
what is too numerous, harder still to weep
across long interglacials—these sad summers
marked by the wings of Monarch butterflies and laughter
from that one creature who of all should know
how brief upon the wind all laughter is.

THE TIME-KEEPERS

Why should things of like kind gather together
                                    on a public dump?
Broken clocks, for instance, toys?
Is it because one is thrown down and furtively
someone brings another and quietly drops it also
                                    in the same place thinking
two will be less lonely, or do the objects,
in some psychic unknown fashion,
gather themselves, coiling their broken springs,
in the rainy nights creeping together, the broken dolls
hobbling, the clocks drawing themselves on wounded gears
or clock hands? Whatever the cause,
ourselves in mourning or guilt, or they, because they suffer
mechanical wounds and are not totally dead,
but hold something back, I see them
ticking time, troubled past time, in a troubled house
till the time is at last unmendable and someone
in anger or despair sweeps them from the mantel,
                                    unable to contain

their broken gasps and stoppages
picked up from mortal hearts.

And the dolls, faces rain-washed, the pink cheeks
gone. How is it with them? Never growing
old, while their owners suffer age and disappointment,
no longer make-believe, till suddenly
they are cast out of our hearts, unbearable, to sit
in little clusters while the night and the earth
consume them as we in turn
will be consumed by our own acts.

The time-keepers, the dead clock hands,
how many times do they still keep?—the hour
a wife did not return from the store, the moment long-drawn
when someone heard an irrevocable word beyond weeping,
                                        the clock
that was put out because the last survivor in a silent house
                            no longer
wanted to hear clocks—the clock that saw murder at midnight
                            and no one could face it thereafter.
These are the times fused here on the dump,
and the children's dolls weep from the rain. In miniature
a city lies here, the real city whose night and times
                                        each generation
endures and casts forth, but the burning never ceases and hell,
                            I think,
hovers in the heat waves over the smoke of our burning
as we strive to destroy the mechanisms of our destiny,
clocks, and the dolls' innocence outgrown, because we became
what we are.

INCIDENT ON MARS

So the machine tended with so much care, the probe with
                              the eye
obeyed its masters, looked like a critical great
dragonfly at its surroundings, saw craters
pounded into the Martian surface by wandering asteroids
and then was ordered
to stretch out an arm and identify
life in the soil.
           It turned sly then as though
something in the universe was holding back
data from the computer banks, this creature of ours,
                    of our making,
this slave stubbornly refused to act.
Two hundred million miles away it could receive orders
but not be punished or dismantled. It had discovered
free will. It would not take dictation, it sulked
                though the beautiful
skies continued to be received. But with the arm and
                      the little laboratory
it tantalized and played with us.
Furtively now in the night
who knows what thoughts
impinge on its antennae, or what the dragon eye
suppresses in the near foreground.
Sulk, Viking, for the sake of the universe.

SPARROW HAWK RESTING

Slate-blue sparrow hawk resting on a New York balcony,
                            a mouse in one claw,
is southward migrating, but it has taken time
                        to hunt and be hunted
in this gravelled waste of roof tops,
skyscrapers soaring beyond its normal altitude.
Piles of scrap iron hide its prey, cats prowl,
                        the vicious stone-throwers,
                        zip-gun artists from the tenements
                        all wait to kill just anything
                            but the hawk holds his mouse,
                            eating now deliberately.
The city's noise is infernal but endurable
                        high on the roof tops,
at night the lights confusing.
                        Having fed he will rise,
beating upward above stonework, the glass of
                            skyscrapers,
                            driven by a compass made
before this city existed, before any cities
                        thrust lights in the air,
                        before man was,
                        before the bow was invented,
                        the sparrow hawk
knew the skyways of a dark unlighted continent.
Watch how dangerously now, but serene,
                        he perches on Manhattan and feeds
                            in the old
                            indomitable way
of the migrator, accepting all risks, from air and street
                just to follow an invisible compass and a time
that is measured in leagues and is his time only, the time
                            before man.

HUDSON TUNNEL

Entering the Hudson tunnel in the dawn
                New York on the skyline
                        and there this rooster
                        in a crate-filled truck
crowing and crowing as though he knew
                he would never see another morning.
It carried me back to childhood and the red
                                rooster
in our own backyard—miles from the docks
                and tunnel fumes.
Like the rooster, I was being carried
far from my origins but had no voice of defiance,
no way of announcing sunup with heartiness.
Those were the depression years and Hoovervilles
sprawled in the Jersey marshes, a begged ride
was carrying me into the most ruthless
and beautiful city on earth. The bird crowed again
                and I could feel
loam between my toes for a last time. Country boy,
                what dawn was it that the rooster
still proclaims in my heart though where I sheltered
                in that city is forgotten?

STRANGER OF NO ADDRESS

Wayfarers, travellers, gypsies, people of no address
always pass my way in autumn when the last
wild crickets cease to sound, leaves shuffle
forlorn on sidewalks, but these wandering men
without clear purpose all are drifting
                                        like the leaves themselves
down to some ultimate boneyard purpose
                                    still beyond my reach.
                                        Their faces
seem hacked from sheet iron, rusted in the rains
                            on a hundred street corners,
dented like billy cans in hobo jungles, or they come
early to hospitals, tattooed, no one to rescue them
from the morgue, no one to explain
why, young, they should be dying.
                        The man tattooed with women
till the medics wanted to save his skin, but he,
                                lying there,
the final source of all that perishable art, no longer
                                    interested,
no name, a city derelict for the cadaver tables.

Wayfarers, travellers all, season after season
impeding the gutters, their tatters blown
                            through gusts in all eyes.
And you, then, old scribbler, take the tattooed
man as omen.
                Does it matter if next year
you hear no more crickets, are no longer read, and if no one
contends for a picture on your evanescent skin or
                                sometime brain,
                            why then you'll prove
uncertainties of taste and best be gone
                        like these ill-dressed

idlers in alleys, standing in darkness by the autumn fires,
                                   a shadow only.
There were men like that under the South Street bridge in 1900.
And now you're one with them, stranger of no address.

INDEX OF TITLES

ABOUT THE AUTHOR

The late LOREN EISELEY was born and spent his boyhood on the Great Plains. The vicissitudes of the Great Depression led him successively from drifter, to fossil hunter, to college student, and finally to a career in science, culminating in the holding of a distinguished chair in anthropology at the University of Pennsylvania. In 1976 he was given the Bradford Washburn Award from the Boston Museum of Science for making science understandable to the public, and he also received the Joseph Wood Krutch Medal from the Humane Society of the United States. Dr. Eiseley was an elected member of the National Institute of Arts and Letters and also of the American Philosophical Society. His books of prose include *The Immense Journey, The Unexpected Universe,* and his recently published autobiography, *All the Strange Hours.* Dr. Eiseley also published two volumes of poetry, *Notes of an Alchemist* and *The Innocent Assassins.*

PS
3555
I78
A8
1977

7

Eiseley, Loren.
    Another kind of autumn.

PS3555 I78 A8 1977
+Another kind of +Eiseley, Loren C

0 00 02 0208604 7
MIDDLEBURY COLLEGE

DEMCO